Passing Ships
A Poetry Between Two Souls Who Met

M.J. Orongan

Ukiyoto Publishing

All global publishing rights are held by

Ukiyoto Publishing

Published in 2023

Content Copyright © M.J. Orongan

ISBN 9789360165307

*All rights reserved.
No part of this publication may be reproduced, transmitted, or stored in a retrieval system, in any form by any means, electronic, mechanical, photocopying, recording or otherwise, without the prior permission of the publisher.*

The moral rights of the authors have been asserted.

This is a work of fiction. Names, characters, businesses, places, events, locales, and incidents are either the products of the author's imagination or used in a fictitious manner. Any resemblance to actual persons, living or dead, or actual events is purely coincidental.

This book is sold subject to the condition that it shall not by way of trade or otherwise, be lent, resold, hired out or otherwise circulated, without the publisher's prior consent, in any form of binding or cover other than that in which it is published.

www.ukiyoto.com

For my special person

Acknowledgement

I wish to express my gratitude to the people who supported me in accomplishing this creation. A word of thank you I would like to say; to the readers who take an interest in this book of poetry, Passing Ships!

I like to express my heartfelt gratitude:
• To my parents Lydia and Ermelando Jr Orongan., who has guided me from day one. To my loving brother Joseph, for your wisdom and suggestions.

• To my friends, colleagues Tin, Karms, Dan, Ly and to my loved ones for believing and supporting me in achieving my dreams.
• To my cousin Rai Espina, for making the illustration.
• To every person who inspired me, your encouragement helps me every step of the way; you guys help me reach my potentials.

• To Ukiyoto Publishing, for helping me in the process of making this book.

• And most of all, to our Almighty God for this privelage to write pages of papers I never could imagine.

Contents

Addiction	1
Bewitched Spirit	2
Come To See Me	3
Grounds Of Hanging On	4
Hallway Fondness	6
In Presence	8
Leaving Town	9
Losing Count	11
Misty Eyes	12
Parallel Universe	13
Passing Ships	14
Seeing You	16
Timely Moments	17
65 Days	18
Haste	20
Scrubs In Teal	22
Stitched	23
Unfinished Business	25
Cordial	26
Coming Times	27

On Thursdays	28
An Exchange Of Words	29
Strangers In The Hallway	30
Ray Of Light	32
Waiting On The Edge	33
Diving Waters	35
Glistening Moonbeams	36
Museum Of Memories	37
Thread	38
Compromising Silence	39
A Pleasant Life	40
Missing Chances	41
Gleaming Pearl	42
Golden Sunshine	43
Unintended	44
Bruised Heart	46
You	47
Coexist	48
Celestial Corpse	49
I Wish	50
Home	51
I Turn Back	52

Let Us Meet	53
Lost And Found	54
Leave	56
Sun Specked Eyes	57
The Resident	58
Distinctive Traits	59
Silhouette	61
Morning And Evening Star	62
Footsteps	63
Crossed Routes	64
Daystar	66
A Little Longer	68
Goodbyes	69
About the Author	71

Addiction

Those eyes of yours
Were like a drug for me
For once, I see your gaze
I became addicted
Wanting to see you more

And when I can't
See you in a day
I became sick
It was the sickness of love
I experience

Bewitched Spirit

Your eyes bewitched
My calm soul
That was so
Magnetically irresistible

Your gaze
Was fiercely mysterious
That makes me fearful
To want to explore you more

Come To See Me

I will come to you
Whenever it is possible to meet you
I will do everything
If it means
To see you in a day

I will say whatever excuses,
I could make of
I would roam around in the stairwells
Going detours
Just to have a glimpse of you

Even if we do not talk to each other
Whether nothing is going on
Between the two of us
Rather than strangers
In the passageway

Grounds Of Hanging On

You were the reason
Why I stayed up at night
Why I did not give up
Working on myself

You were the reason why
I stayed and continued to
Persevere in helping
The people in need

You were the sole reason
Why I am
Still here
Living this life of mine

Without you
I will be gone

Completely isolated
Forbidden to enter the world I used to live

Hallway Fondness

When I got out of the room
I saw you standing
Waiting for someone
In the middle of the hallway

I took the courage to step forward
Founding myself standing beside you
Hearing your voice
That was centimeters aways from my ears
So deep and soothing to perceive

Yet, I did not feel rambling butterflies in my stomach
Neither do I hear a piece of music
That most people say
When you fall in love

Rather
I felt comfortable, safe, and secured
Like I finally found someone
Who I can call home

In Presence

Love,
Even if I don't see your
Large lustrous eyes
That keeps me safe and calm

Even if I don't see your
Smile so genuinely sweet
Even if I don't hear your
Euphonious voice

Even if I don't see your
Defensively wide stance
It is still you whom
My heart and mind go to

Leaving Town

I needed to see you
One more time
Before I leave
The town

So I grab the opportunity
To come to you
Even if it is
Already late

And there you are
Standing humbly
Talking comfortably and professionally
To someone

I am glad that my
Prayer to see you

Passing Ships

Is granted in

A short amount of time

Losing Count

I lost count
Of the days
That you were gone
And not by my side anymore

I feel numb
And somehow
Stuck in the life
That I am living

But I have
To continue
The journey of life
Not only for me but also
For us

Misty Eyes

As the rain
Falls from the sky
So thus
My tears
Dropping from my eyes

Crying out
All the feelings
That was deeply
Horrid and delightful
Sentimental memories of you and I

Parallel Universe

Maybe in another universe
You and I exist
Living a joyous life
Creating unforgettable memories
And not a life full of pain and misery

In another interplanetary space
You and I exist
As we build our family
A home
Full of love

But not in this void above
Not at this time
Not in this lifetime
Not in this world
And especially not in this metagalactic space

Passing Ships

Looking at you
Going inside your car
While I was going out in my car
Made me think
That we are two souls passing by

Souls who were connected and
Linked together by chain
You were a soul which I can feel
That you were near and beside me
But you, typically were not

Each opportunity to take a glance
Of your beauty, I took
Each second that passed by
To gaze at your stance
I took

Each time to
Have a chance to walk near you
I took it beacause
There was nothing like you
For you made me a guided path of
Where I am destined to go

Seeing You

Seeing the view of your back
Suddenly let me feel
More alive
Even if
I am in lack sleep

Seeing you walking
In an uphill ramp
On your way
To the corridors
Full of people waiting

And seeing you
In my dreams
Each morning and night
Helped me survive
Throughout the day

Timely Moments

You came to me
In such great
Unexpected moments
Where I did not prepare myself
Physically and emotionally

You came out of the blue
Whether it may be
In the form of biometric technology
Or in the hallways
Or in my dreams

You came in front of me
Without prior notice
You came unpredictably into my life
And you walk away
Like a perfect stranger

65 Days

65 days before
I saw you physically again
Where many things
Have changed

In that certain period
We are
Separated
From one another

I could not further express
The happiness I felt today
To see your eyes
To have a glimpse of you once again

Even if
It is just

In a split second of
Looking at your existence

Haste

What must have
I done
To let you treat me this way
Wherein every time I walk near you or
When the time I take a glimpse of you or
When I try to enunciate words

You tended to walk out of my sight
Right away
You walked fastly paced
Acting that you are busy
When, in fact
There's none to be, hurried with

You let me felt
As if I am guilt
Of your actions

And wonder
What did I do wrong all this time
That you no longer seek for me

Scrubs In Teal

In your teal scrubs, you wore
At night were I close my eyes
You come to me
In speak of good news
News that would make me breathe
To sustain the life I desired for long

In your teal scrubs, you wore
In your hands which opened the door
For possibilities of
You and I might be together
On the grounds of heavens
And not here on earth

Stitched

I remember the time
Where you and I crossed paths
In a room where you did your rounds
And you come to notice my presence
You speak to me and seems
To know what my profession was

Your words were floating in the air
When I come to realize
That my mouth could not utter a single word
So I turn my back on you
Wiping away the sweat running down my face
And when I turned at you
It was too late to say a word

And ever since that day
Regrets have been, always formed in my mind

I think of what-ifs. and
What?
And it haunts and burns me down to this day.

Unfinished Business

This
Is where
I leave you now

For I think
I have finished
My role

In coming to your life
And you
Coming into mine

If we see each other again
Then I guess my role has
Not yet ended

Cordial

You knew
My profession
As you speak in a
Cordial manner
And it left me
Completely speechless
Losing my opportunity
To talk to you

Coming Times

Out of all the men
I admired
You were the only one
Whom I envisioned
To build
My future with

But fate has a different path
For both of us
To go
In a separate way
Where we can
Build our future with another partner

On Thursdays

If there is ever one day
I could choose to
Look forward to
It will be on the fourth day of the week
As it will be the time
To have a glimpse of you
In situations where I least
Expected, you the most

An Exchange Of Words

A request is
Heard from above
To aspire a talk
Between two people

Where one
Is greatly in love
And the other
Is not

A conversation
Where one longed for
The longest time has come true
In formal visions and not in actuality

Strangers In The Hallway

I dreamt of you
Concerning my current relationship and
How can I go home knowing that
My current partner is cheating on me

I dreamt of you standing
Holding a baby
While I was sitting
On an old cushioned chair

I dreamt of you cradling
Lovingly
With all your heart
That your life depends on it

I dreamt of you and
You alone and

I wish it is the reality
Of how things should end for the both of us

But I was living
In my fantasy world
A vision far away from reality
For we are strangers in the hallway

Ray Of Light

You were a new ray of light
Of my life's darkened walls
You brought me smiles and
Winks during the day
Where my eyes squinted for
Me to see

You were my hope
My sun
Brightly shining
In my skies
Leaving my energies and emotions stronger than
I will never know

Waiting On The Edge

If you were the sun and
I, the sky
The sets will
Never be known
And only every rise
Will I ever seek

I will drift away
Through the edge of the
Ocean and greens
Waiting for you
To shine your way
Towards me

And by then
I will be greater, better than
What I am today

For I mostly glowed
Whenever I am with you

Diving Waters

I would have dived myself,
Into the world of writing
If you also dived
Yourself,
With me

Pouring all these emotions and
Leave, it
Beneath
The waters of
Mystery

And by the time we rose
From the sea above
I hope you and I
Could replenish such scented memories
Starting a new

Glistening Moonbeams

Our eyes entwined
On a summer day
Where it lingered a few seconds longer
Where your soul somehow
Captured mine

Listening to your whispering voice
Summons me
To write a poetry
During midnight and
Glistening moonbeams

Longing for your breaths and sighs
Your gaze, your smile, your voice
Now and then
Make me more in love
With these devoted sensations

Museum Of Memories

You gave me a ton
Of museum memories
Whether in reality or
In dreamy frames

You gave me bountiful and
Joyous moments
That I could retrieve
Any time of the day

You gave me life
As what your profession used to be
And I wanted to
Express my heartfelt gratitude
To you, my dearest divine

Thread

Where did it all begin?
They asked
I answered
It began with a glimpse
He was there everywhere I go
And sometimes
He was nowhere to be found

But I hold
A woolen thread
Woven with a connected string of red
So that whenever either of us was
Lost
We could find each other again
Somewhere in time

Compromising Silence

To feel this way
And
Say nothing
Whenever I am with you

Was
A painful feeling to endure
Which, was why
Writing these words

Thus serve to
Compromise
My silence
To all the days
I was near you

A Pleasant Life

How pleasant life must be
When I live with you
To watch the leafy trees
Swaying with the foursome winds
Of the window chambers

With the light of yours
You open not only the
Bright blue skies of mine
But also the sun, stars, and
Moon

Missing Chances

Out in the sea
Are two ships sailing by
When a strong wind came up
It said
"A room you shall make, Mist"

Hailing both ships
Sailing on away, they cried
As night banned out and
Sun is nearly awake
They missed their chances

Gleaming Pearl

Far out in the
Clear crystal, sea
Deeper you swam
Breaking my coral walls
Shattering the clear windows of amber and
Disintegrating the Mussell shelled roofs

You descended
To see a shell
A gleaming pearl
As you search for a partner
That will fit your
Royal crown

Golden Sunshine

I once was told
To not fly near the sun for
I will be
Melted
Like a wax

But I winged myself
Anyways
To feel the free blows of
Bluish air
Wheeling and soaring

So high I went
To meet my golden sunshine
And in his blazing heat
I softened and found myself
Floating in the waves of ground

Unintended

You were; never meant to be mine
To begin with
You already belonged to someone
And
I was; never meant to be yours
For someone
Already owned me

Our story
Was never meant to meet
Our story
Was never meant to tell
Our story
Was never meant to be written

Yet,
I forced things

For the people to know
The story of us

Bruised Heart

You are healing

From the traumas and struggles

You encountered

Of the past

And

So was I

I guess we passed

Each other

To patch our

Bruised hearts

To mourn together

And renew ourselves

You

You brought light
In my grey skies
You heated me up
On my chilly nights

You let me breathe
When my lungs collapsed
You let me find myself
When I was lost

You were my
Guardian, an angel
From the land of promise
And not in the extraterrestrials

Coexist

I hope we
Could live on a planet
Where the sun and moon
Day and night
Oceans below and above
Coexist together

For by then
We will never have to be afraid
Of losing one another
For by then
We will never have to
Part our ways again

Celestial Corpse

I will die
Along the celestial corpses
In the galaxy
If I have to
Come near your sunbeams
That could burn
My entire being

I will die
Along with the celestial corpses
In the galaxy
If I have to come and chase you
In the universal world
That could let me
Out of breath

I Wish

I wish
You are the
Sea
That calls
A young sailor back

I wish
You are the
Waves
That lead my ship
Float towards you

I wish that
You search for me
As I search for you
In my dreams

Home

My core screams
For your name
In reverberating chambers
It echoes continuously
That it could not be
Suddenly stopped

My foot stumbles
Where I fell onto a rocky ground
My hands are in a tremendous state
Whenever we cross paths
In the crowded streets

I am afraid to commit but
At the same time
I am at peace
For you are my captain
Who brought me back home

I Turn Back

I kept on turning
To see your dazzling eyes
To look at your radiant smile
To look at you wholesomely
Once more

I kept on turning
My back
To see your
Precious beauty
For the second time

But then
When I look back at you
For the third time
I lost sight of you
You are gone

Let Us Meet

Let us meet
In the blue hour
After the sun melts down
Into the horizons

Let me see how your
Beautiful soul
Is perfectly made
Let me feel how your
Energy blooms

Let us meet
Where people see the
Shores and land
To tell them what our story is

Lost And Found

I was lost

In the storm

Raging in blackened destruction

I was lost

In the woods

Where the ashen peaks touch the skies

I was stranded

In the blaming wildfire

Stuck in the middle of nowhere

I did not know what else to do

But to

Stand with a confused mind

Then,

I found you

A glimpse of light

I see from afar
Bringing me hope, wisdom, and will
To find my way back home

Leave

I miss you when you are away
But could not express it
Whenever you are near

I longed to see you
For days and a couple of months
But could not
Let words flow by

So, I ask you to leave.
Because to wait this long and
Love you from afar
I am content

Sun Specked Eyes

To come across with you
Through these winding streets
Creating new intricate stories

To see the world
Through the eyes of a sun-specked individual
Uncovering my true self is
Truly a pleasure of mine

As we journey along and
Separate our ways
May we relive the days
That had gone by

The Resident

You've become a permanent resident
Not only in my mind but
In all of my body organs
Sending echoes and alarms
Throughout the entire system
All the time

A game of tug and war
I've undergone the whole time
And asked the person in me
Whether
To let you stay in my thoughts
Or is it time for me to let go?

Distinctive Traits

Your personality is quite **j**ovial
And **o**dd in some other ways
In your line of work,
I found your **s**incerity and **e**fficiency
Which I adore

A **p**ioneer who is willing to **a**dapt
To life **o**pen-heartedly
A **l**ad
Who is **o**ptimistic enough,
To have plans for the future

You are **g**racious, **a**dventurous, and **r**adiant
You are **c**harming, I must say
A very **i**mpressive
Abstract art
That I could not understand

But I want to hold in my possession

All these distinctive traits
I see in a human form
A precious piece
That I could not let go easily

Silhouette

I watch your black silhouette
Slowly disappear
On an open sky

With me
Being left
Alone in a ship of strangers
I felt my bones ache and
My lungs draw for a breath

How can I stop this agony
I face
Reminiscing the encounters
In a gallery of one

Morning And Evening Star

In our world
You will be my morning star
And I will be
The evening star

In our world
We don't have to worry
About a thing or two
Because it will be the only
Two of us

Footsteps

You hurried your footsteps.
Because someone
Needed your service
But deep inside
I hope you are on your way
Because you knew
I was there

Crossed Routes

On the day
That I promised myself
To let go of you completely
Cannot be astonishingly fulfilled

For
The next day
I still say my good mornings
And goodbyes
From the image I have seen
Whenever I passed by

How can I possibly
Let go of you in just one day?
Among the countless days
We crossed paths

How can I possibly
Let you go
When all there is
In my mind and soul were you?

Daystar

You are like the sun.
That gives creatures
To survive
In the wild

When an individual's brain is in
A state of the confused, foggy place
You brought clarity
To the thick clouds above them

You are the daylight.
That gives your
Patients' peace and confidence
In their hearts

May this sunny necklace
Remind you that you are

The day star
That brings hope in their darkest days

A Little Longer

I wish you stare at me longer
Like how you
Fixed your gaze
To the present
I gave

I wish
I can see your bright smile
A little longer
On the day
You receive it

I wish you searched and
Wait
For me
A little bit more
To introduce myself to you

Goodbyes

This

Is goodbye

To the person I met

To the one who fits the

Thousand tiny puzzle pieces of me

This

Is goodbye

To the person who brought

Warmness on my rainy days

Wrapping me with a hug

When my world is about to collapse

This

Is farewell

To the person whom

I tend to propose

My golden sunshine
My bliss

About the Author

M.J. Orongan

M.J. attain a degree in Occupational Therapy at Cebu Doctors' University. She works as an Occupational Therapist helping people with disabilities and children with special needs in achieving quality of life. She is a blog contributor, a co-author of poetry anthologies in India, and a writer based in Cebu, Philippines. Her hobbies include doing arts and crafts, lyric writing, listening to classical music, watching action movies, reading poetry books, and painting during her pastime. Penning her feelings and thoughts into words and forming a story from broken fragments is to show her creativity to inspire others. She believes that through her writings, one can become an immortal being. Whether here on earth or in the heavens above. Furthermore, she started her Instagram page @*moonstoneblues98* in the past two (2) years.

www.ingramcontent.com/pod-product-compliance
Lightning Source LLC
LaVergne TN
LVHW041221080526
838199LV00082B/1800